Super Bowl Champions: New York Giants

Linebacker Lawrence Taylor

Wide receiver Sterling Shepard

SUPER BOWL CHAMPIONS

NEW YORK GIANTS

MICHAEL E. GOODMAN

CREATIVE SPORTS

CREATIVE EDUCATION / CREATIVE PAPERBACKS

Published by Creative Education and Creative Paperbacks
P.O. Box 227, Mankato, Minnesota 56002
Creative Education and Creative Paperbacks are imprints of
The Creative Company
www.thecreativecompany.us

Design and production by Blue Design (www.bluedes.com)
Art direction by Rita Marshall

Photographs by Alamy (dpa picture alliance, Tribune
Content Agency LLC), AP Images (ASSOCIATED PRESS),
Getty Images (Bill Cummings/WireImages.com, New York
Daily News Archive, NFL Photos, Robert Riger, Joe Robbins,
Jamie Sabau, Jamie Squire, Damian Strohmeyer, Rob
Tringali/SportsChrome, Tim Warner), Unsplash.com (Keith
Champaco)

Library of Congress Cataloging-in-Publication Data
Names: Goodman, Michael E., author.
Title: New York Giants / Michael E. Goodman.
Includes bibliographical references and index.
Summary: Approachable text and engaging photos
    highlight the New York Giants' Super Bowl wins and
    losses, plus sensational players associated with the team
    such as Michael Strahan.
Identifiers: LCCN 2021044420 | ISBN 9781640263970
    (library binding) | ISBN 9781628329308 (paperback) | ISBN
    9781640005617 (ebook)
Subjects: LCSH: New York Giants (Football team)—Juvenile
    literature.
Classification: LCC GV956.N4 G643 2023 (print) | LCC GV956.
    N4 (ebook) | DDC 796.332/64097471—dc23

Wide receiver David Tyree

Defensive end Olivier Vernon

CONTENTS

Home of the Giants

ew York City is the largest city in the United States. It has many **skyscrapers**, restaurants, and theaters. It also has two professional football teams. One is called the Giants. They have been playing football in New York since 1925.

The Giants are part of the National Football League (NFL). All the teams in the NFL try to win the Super Bowl. The winner is the champion of the league. As of 2021, the Giants have played in five Super Bowls. They have won four of them.

Wide receiver Odell Beckham Jr.

Naming the Giants

The Giants first played at the Polo Grounds. A top baseball team called the Giants also played there. The owner decided to give his club the same name. He hoped his team would be just as successful.

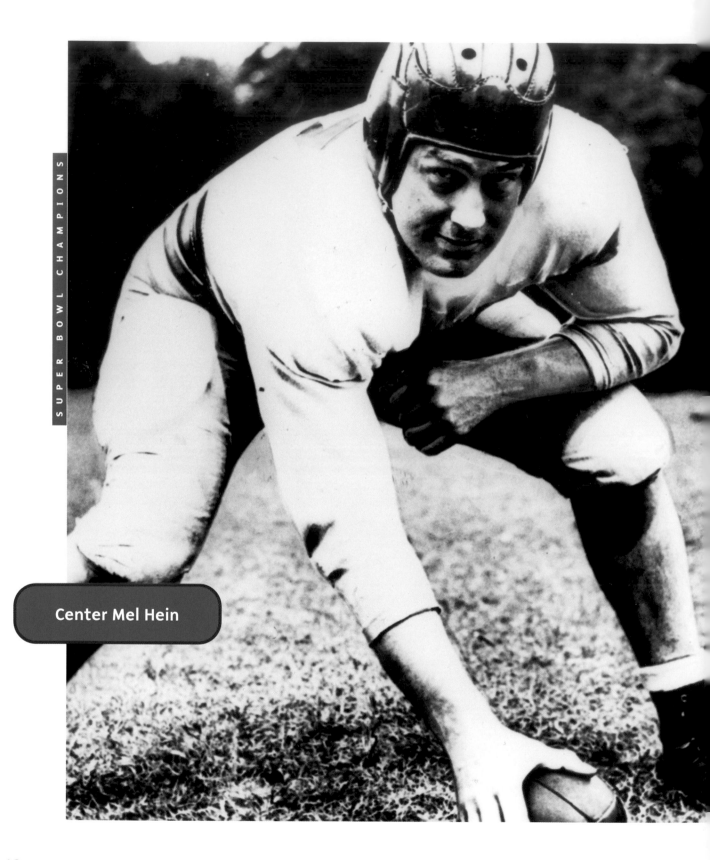

Center Mel Hein

Giants History

The Giants began playing in 1925. They got off to a quick start. The club won the NFL championship in only its third season! The Giants won two more **titles** in 1934 and 1938.

Mel Hein was the first big star in New York. He played center on **offense** and linebacker on **defense**. He played every minute of every game for 15 years!

The Giants won many games in the 1950s and 1960s. Fans cheered for quarterback Charlie Conerly and halfback Frank Gifford. The Giants won a third title in 1956. They played in five more NFL championship games in the next seven years.

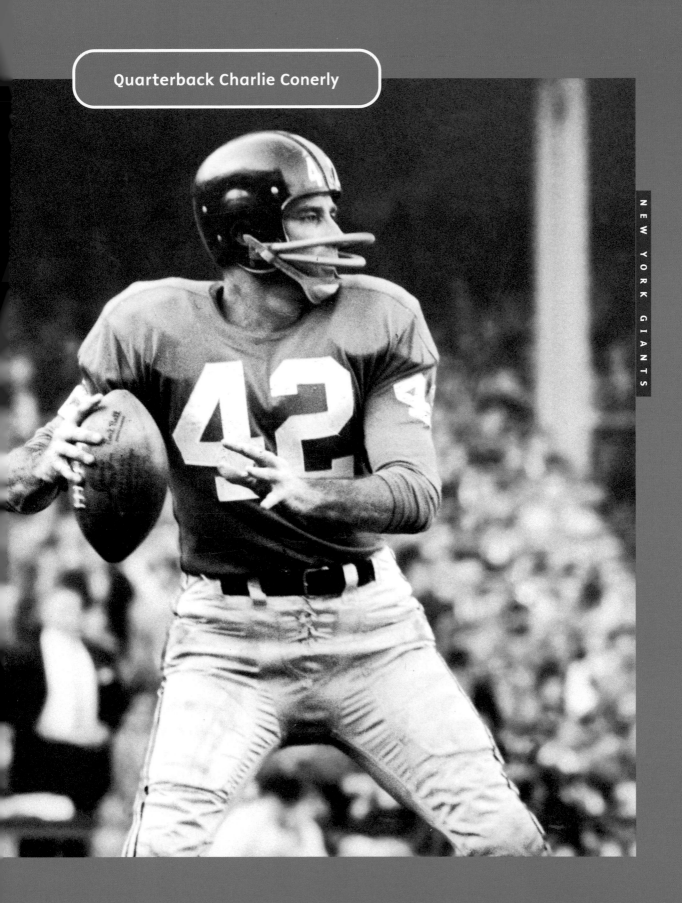

Quarterback Charlie Conerly

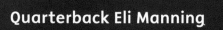

Quarterback Eli Manning

In the 1980s, smart quarterback Phil Simms ran the Giants' offense. He was an **accurate** passer. The team's star on defense was tough linebacker Lawrence Taylor. The Giants won Super Bowls after the 1986 and 1990 seasons.

New York did not win any more titles in the 1990s. **Clutch** quarterback Eli Manning joined the team in 2004. He led the Giants to comeback wins in Super Bowls XLII (42) and XLVI (46).

Other Giants Stars

Running back Tiki Barber was quick and strong. He gained more yards than any other Giants runner. Michael Strahan was a star defensive end. In 2001, he set an NFL **record** by making 22.5 **sacks**.

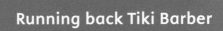
Running back Tiki Barber

Running back Saquon Barkley

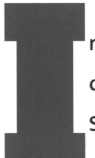**I**n 2018 and 2019, the Giants added powerful running back Saquon Barkley and quick quarterback Daniel Jones. Fans hope the young players will lead the team to many more titles.

About the Giants

Started playing: 1925

. . . .

Conference/division: National Football Conference, East Division

. . . .

Team colors: blue and red

. . . .

Home stadium: MetLife Stadium

. . . .

SUPER BOWL VICTORIES:

XXI, January 25, 1987, 39–20 over Denver Broncos

. . . .

XXV, January 27, 1991, 20–19 over Buffalo Bills

. . . .

XLII, February 3, 2008, 17–14 over New England Patriots

. . . .

XLVI, February 5, 2012, 21–17 over New England Patriots

. . . .

New York Giants website: www.giants.com

. . . .

Glossary

accurate — on target

....

clutch — playing well under pressure

....

defense — the players who try to keep the other team from scoring

....

offense — the players who control the ball and try to score

....

record — top performances that are better than anyone else has done

....

sacks — tackles of a quarterback who is trying to throw a pass

....

skyscrapers — tall, narrow buildings that have at least 10 stories, or levels

....

titles — in sports, another word for championships

....

Wide receiver Victor Cruz

Index